# SEASONAL BOOKS

# THE SANDMAN
## SEASON 1

Alex Garcia

# TABLE OF CONTENTS


Part 1: Synthesis                          5

Part 2: Notable crew and cast              11

Part 3: Quick episode guide                21

Part 4: Detailed episode guide             23

# PART 1
# SYNTHESIS

The first season of *The Sandman* adapts for the small screen the first eighteen issues of the Vertigo comic book series (excluding #9). In doing so, it offers some of the most breath-taking visuals ever shot for television. The opening of the premiere episode alone is quite promising and heralds great things to come.

The plotline concerns Morpheus, the king of dreams and one of the Endless, who after being held prisoner for over a century attempts to restore the Dreaming to its former glory. To achieve this, he must retrieve his stolen tools: a helm, a ruby, and a pouch of sand.

Another vital player is the Corinthian. An escaped nightmare who acts as a serial killer in the real world. Dream was about to undo him when he was captured by Sir Roderick Burgess, aka Magus. Hoping to preserve his own freedom, the Corinthian informs Burgess on his prisoners's true nature and how to keep him bound.

Neil Gaiman has been one of the most creative authors of the past five decades—whether as a novelist or as a comic book writer. His work on the Sandman was an early highlight of his career, that helped throw him into the limelight.

In the first season, Morpheus first appears as a cold, distant, uncompromising, god-like being who would remain a prisoner for 106 years rather than give in to his captor's demands. By the end of the season, however, he has evolved quite a bit. Along the way, he learns humility and that he, too, despite his nature, needs friendship and love in his life.

We see hints of this throughout the series, starting as early as the second episode. After having escaped from his prison but greatly weakened by his captivity and the loss of his tools, Morpheus must feed on his creation to gain some power. He does this by sucking the essence of Abel and Cain's pet gargoyle, leaving the two brothers heartbroken. While he shows little compassion or remorse when destroying the creature, in the end he sends them a new baby gargoyle to replace the previous one.

In the fifth episode, despite John's actions, Morpheus takes pity on the man. Rather than kill him, he makes him slip into a long-term sleep.

The most significant change, however, occurs after he meets up with his sister Death in "The sound of her wings" (episode #6). Watching her work, he sees the compassion and love she has for those she takes. And then he is reminded of a man he first met with her in 1389, a man Death agreed to make immortal so her brother could meet him once every hundred years. Though his initial goal was to prove a point—that humans would hate living such a long life—he now realizes that the ritual has turned into something else entirely.

The interesting thing is that if Morpheus hadn't gone through all these changes, it is quite likely the season would have ended quite differently. But Morpheus is now a more compassionate being—more 'human' if you would—and so his actions reflect this.

Speaking of the end, it spreads across two intense episodes set at a "cereal convention" (really a *serial killer* convention). There, the Corinthian tries to talk Rose Walker into destroying Dream and the Dreaming—which she has the power to do because of her nature as a Vortex. But there is grave danger in this, as it would affect the waking world as well.

A bonus episode was released that includes two stories in one: a short animated feature where cats dream of a world where they once ruled; and another where the muse Calliope is held prisoner—much like Dream was—so she can inspire her captor.

With all this, *The Sandman* is an engaging show that manages to thrill and surprise, while remaining faithful to the source material. It has stunning visuals with powerful and emotional messaging, and a stellar ensemble cast.


## HIGHLIGHT EPISODES

Though all episodes are of high quality, there are a few that still manage to stand out.

- #5 "24/7": With Dream's ruby in his possession, John walks into a diner and wishes for all the patrons to speak only the truth. This brings out all the ugliness in people's lives and little by little things deteriorate, leading to a string of murders and suicides.

- #6 "The sound of her wings": Morpheus walks with Death, watching her work, then remembers an immortal human he meets once a century.

◆ #9-10 "Collectors" & "Lost hearts": The serial killer convention is a brilliant idea for a setting. It takes place in a hotel, amid guests (and personnel) who have no clue what is really going on.

# PART 2
# NOTABLE CREW AND CAST

Seven directors and twelve writers worked on the first eleven episodes of *The Sandman*.

Mike Barker (ep. #1) is a British director who made a name for himself with the 2003 feature film "To kill a king." He has since directed episodes of many British and American TV shows, including *Silent witness*, *Broadchurch*, *Outlander*, *Fargo*, and *The handmaid's tale*.

Jamie Childs (eps. #2-5) is another British director. He has shot episodes of *Doctor Who*, *His dark materials*, and *Willow*.

Mairzee Almas (ep. #6) is a Canadian citizen who began her career as an actress and an assistant director. She has been an episodic director for three decades, working on shows such as *Smallville*, *Haven*, *The 100*, *Defiance*, *Lucifer*, *Arrow*, *Impulse*, *Outlander*, and *Paper girls*.

Andrés Baiz (eps. #7-8) was born in Colombia. After directing feature films and TV shows in his country, he had the opportunity to work on *Narcos* and *Narcos: Mexico*.

Coralie Fargeat (ep. #9) is a French writer and director, best known for her debut feature film "Revenge" from 2017. *The Sandman* was her first venture in American television.

Louise Hooper (eps. #10-11) is known for her work on British medical soaps *Doctors*, *Holby City*, and *Casualty*. She has also shot episodes of *Cold feet*, *Cheat*, and *The Witcher*.

Hisko Hulsing (ep. #11 part 1) is a Dutch animator. He animated sequences of the 2014 Kurt Cobain documentary and directed some animated shorts. He also directed and production designed Amazon's first adult cartoon *Undone* in 2019.

Neil Gaiman (ep. #1) is best known as a novelist and as the creator of the *Sandman* comic book for Vertigo (DC Comics). Some of his novels have been adapted into movies ("Stardust") or TV shows (*American gods*, *Good omens*...). He is also a screenwriter, with several features ("MirrorMask," "Beowulf") and TV episodes (most notably for *Babylon 5* and *Doctor Who*) to his credit. He also played himself in an episode of *The Big Bang theory* and his voice can be heard in ep. #11 of *The Sandman*.

David S. Goyer (ep. #1) has been working in film and television for four decades. His credits include the movies "Dark City," "Blade" (and its two sequels), Christopher Nolan's "Dark Knight" trilogy, "Jumper," and "Man of steel." For the small screen, he created, wrote, and produced *Sleepwalkers*, *FreakyLinks*, *Blade: the series*, *FlashForward*, *Da Vinci's demons*, *Constantine*, and he more recently developed the TV adaptation of Isaac Asimov's *Foundation*.

Allan Heinberg (eps. #1-2) has written episodes of *Party of five*, *Sex and the city*, *The O.C.*, *Grey's anatomy*, *Scandal*, and *The catch*. In 2017 he wrote the screenplay for Patty Jenkins' hit film "Wonder Woman" starring Gal Gadot as the title character.

Jim Campolongo (ep. #3) has worked on *White collar*, *Graceland*, *The blacklist*, and *The catch*.

Austin Guzman's (ep. #4) previous credits include *Grey's anatomy*, *Why women kill*, and *Scandal*.

Ameni Rozsa (ep. #5) had previously written episodes of *Complications*, *The catch*, *Scandal*, *The right stuff*, and *Yellowjackets*.

Lauren Bello (ep. #6) worked as an assistant to Goyer on *Da Vinci's demons* and *Krypton*. She became a writer on *Foundation* and is also credited as a story editor on *The Sandman*.

Heather Bellson (ep. #7) is no stranger to Gaiman's work as she had previously written for *American gods*. Other credits include *Black sails* and *The walking dead*.

Alexander Newman-Wise (ep. #8) was a writer on *The catch* and *For the people*.

Vanessa James Benton (ep. #9) was on the production staff of *In contempt* and *How to get away with murder* (for which she wrote one episode) before joining *The Sandman* as a staff writer.

Jay Franklin (ep. #10) was a segment producer for *The Daily Show* before joining the production staff of *For the people*. Before *The Sandman*, he had written an episode of *Briarpatch*. He is also credited as a writers' assistant.

Catherine Smyth-McMullen (ep. #11) has been a writers' assistant for several years and worked in the costume department on *The leftovers*. She is also credited as a staff writer.

* * *


The show's first season counts fifteen notable guest stars—some in recurring roles, others in tiny ones.

Charles Dance (ep. #1) opens the festivities with his dark and powerful portrayal of Sir Roderick Burgess, aka "Magus." He is, of course, best known for his role as Tywin Lannister in *Game of thrones*. His career, however, spans six decades, with numerous credits in film and television, including *Father Brown* (1974), "For your eyes only" (1981), *The professionals* (1983), *The jewel and the crown* (1984), *Tales of the unexpected* (1987), *Mission: impossible* (1989), "Alien 3" (1992), "Last action hero" (1993), *Foyle's war* (2002), *Merlin* (2009), "Ghostbusters" (2016), and "Godzilla: King of the monsters" (2019).

Jenna Coleman plays Johanna Constantine (eps. #2-3, 6). *Doctor Who* fans will remember her as the beloved Clara Oswald (the "impossible girl"). She is also well-known as Jasmine Thomas, a character she played in 180 episodes of the British soap opera *Emmerdale*. She was also in nine episodes of *Waterloo Road*, and played Connie in "Captain America: The first Avenger" (2011).

Joely Richardson is Ethel Dee (eps. #2-3, 5). She was a regular on the popular *Nip/Tuck* (2003-2010), played Queen Catherine in *The Tudors* (2010) and Glinda in the Oz-inspired *Emer-*

*ald City* (2017). She was also in two episodes of *The blacklist*. Her feature credits include "101 Dalmatians" (1996), "Event Horizon" (1997), and "The girl with the dragon tattoo" (2011).

David Thewlis as John Dee (eps. #2-5). Best known for his role as Remus Lupin in the "Harry Potter" franchise, he also played Joby in Terry Gilliam's "The zero theorem" (2013) and Sir Patrick / Ares in "Wonder Woman" and "Justice League" (2017). For television, he has appeared in ten episodes of *Fargo* and had regular voice roles on animated shows *Big mouth* and *Human resources*.

Gwendoline Christie as Lucifer Morningstar (eps. #4, 10). Gained worldwide recognition through the Brienne of Tarth character she played on *Game of thrones*. She was seen in Terry Gilliam's "The Imaginarium of Doctor Parnassus" (2009) and "The zero theorem" (2013). She also played Captain Phasma in the "Star Wars" franchise. In 2012, she joined the main cast of British series *Wizards vs aliens* and played school principal Larissa Weems in the first season of *Wednesday* (2022).

Ian McNeice, who plays a bartender (ep. #6), is a British actor with a long career behind him. He first came to prominence in 1985 playing agent Harcourt on *Edge of darkness*. Other television work includes guest starring roles in episodes of *Minder* (1984), *Lovejoy* (1991), *Inspector Morse* (1993), *Cadfael* (1996), *Jonathan Creek* (2010), and *Foundation* (2021). He played Baron Harkonnen in the 2000 *Dune* miniseries and Winston Churchill in 4 episodes of *Doctor Who* (2010-2011). Additionally, he was a regular on *Doc Martin* (2004-2022) and *Rome* (2005-2007). On the big screen, he can be spotted in such films as "Top secret!" (1984), "The Russia House" (1990), "The Englishman who went up a hill but came down a mountain" (1995), and "From Hell" (2001).

Stephen Fry plays Gilbert aka Fiddler's Green (eps. #7, 9-10). Best known as one half of the Fry and Laurie comedy duo. He's played in numerous films, including "A fish called Wanda" (1988), "Gosford Park" (2001), Neil Gaiman's "MirrorMask" (2005), "V for Vendetta" (2006), Tim Burton's "Alice in Wonderland" (2010) as the voice of the Cheshire Cat, and the two "Hobbit" movies (2013-14). On television, he was a regular on the British *Blackadder* series (1986-99), had a recurring part on *Bones* (2007-2017), and also guest starred on *The new statesman* (1989), *24* (2014), *Doctor Who* (2020), and *The*

*Simpsons* (2021). He also played the title character in *Kingdom* (2007-2009).

Mark Hamill voices Mervyn Pumpkinhead (eps. #7, 9). Best known as Luke Skywalker from the "Star Wars" franchise, he also played in "Slipstream" (1989), "Sleepwalkers" (1992), and "Village of the damned" (1995). He began his career in television, guest starring on *The Partridge family*, *Cannon*, *Night gallery*, *The F.B.I.*, *Bronk*, *The streets of San Francisco*, and numerous other shows. Aside from his acting, he has also lent his voice to video games and animated films and series, including the Joker in several *Batman* cartoons. He also voiced Chucky in the 2019 remake of "Child's play."

Lenny Henry as the voice of Martin Tenbones (eps. #8, 10). A British actor and stand-up comedian. He has appeared in episodes of *Broadchurch* (2017) and *Doctor Who* (2020). He had a recurring role as Sadoc Burrows on *The Lord of the Rings: The rings of power* (2022).

Sandra Oh, who plays the voice of the cat prophet (ep. #11), is best known for her starring roles in *Arliss* (1996-2002), *Grey's anatomy* (2005-2014), and *Killing Eve* (2018-2022). She also guest starred in episodes of *Popular* (1999),

*Judging Amy* (2001), *Six feet under* (2001), and *American crime* (2017)

Scottish actor James McAvoy voices the golden-haired man (ep. #11). He is perhaps best known for his role as Mr. Tumnus in the first "Narnia" film (2005). Other notable parts include a younger version of Prof. Xavier in the "X-Men" franchise and a starring role in M. Night Shyamalan's "Split" (2016). He was also a regular on *His dark materials* (2019-2022).

David Tennant plays the voice of Don (ep. #11). He is best known as the tenth and fourteenth Doctors in *Doctor Who*. He also starred in *Broadchurch* (2013-17), *Gracepoint* (2014), *Good omens* (2019), and *Around the world in 80 days* (2021).

Michael Sheen voices Paul (ep. #11). He played in "Kingdom of Heaven" (2005) and Tim Burton's "Alice in Wonderland" (2010). Perhaps best known for his roles as Lucian in the "Underworld" franchise and Aro in the "Twilight saga." On the small screen, he has guest starred on *Doctor Who* (2011) and *The Simpsons* (2017), among other shows. He was a regular on *Masters of sex* (2013-16), *Good omens* (2017), and *Prodigal son* (2019-21).

Nonso Anozie, who voices the wyvern (ep. #11), has had major roles in "Ender's game" (2013) and Kenneth Branagh's "Cinderella" (2015). Notable roles in television include Xaro Xhoan Daxos in *Game of thrones* (2012), R.M. Renfield on *Dracula* (2013-14) and Abraham Kenyatta on *Zoo* (2015-17). He also guest starred in an episode of *Doctor Who* (2015) and played the lead role in *Sweet tooth* (2021).

Derek Jacobi as author Erasmus Fry (ep. #11). A British actor with a long career in film and television. He started in the 60s, appearing in episodes of *Armchair theatre* and *ITV Playhouse*. Film work includes "The Odessa File" (1974), "The Medusa Touch" (1978), Kenneth Branagh's "Henry V" (1989) and "Dead again" (1991), Ridley Scott's "Gladiator" (2000), and "Tomb raider" (2018). On television, he guest starred in episodes of *Minder* (1979), *Tales of the unexpected* (1980-82), *The storyteller* (1990), *Frasier* (2001), *Doctor Who* (2007), *The Borgias* (2011), and *Good omens* (2019). He is perhaps best known for starring as *Cadfael* (1994-98).

# PART 3
# QUICK EPISODE GUIDE

1 (1-1) Sleep of the Just
>**prod.** #T13.22351. **Aired** 5 Aug 22.
>**Dir:** Mike Barker.
>**Writ:** Neil Gaiman, David S. Goyer & Allan Heinberg.

2 (1-2) Imperfect hosts
>**prod.** #T13.22352. **Aired** 5 Aug 22.
>**Dir:** Jamie Childs. **Writ:** Allan Heinberg.

3 (1-3) Dream a little dream of me
>**prod.** #T13.22353. **Aired** 5 Aug 22.
>**Dir:** Jamie Childs. **Writ:** Jim Campolongo.

4 (1-4) A hope in Hell
>**prod.** #T13.22354. **Aired** 5 Aug 22.
>**Dir:** Jamie Childs. **Writ:** Austin Guzman.

5 (1-5) 24/7
>**prod.** #T13.22355. **Aired** 5 Aug 22.
>**Dir:** Jamie Childs. **Writ:** Ameni Rozsa.

6 (1-6) The sound of her wings
>**prod.** #T13.22356. **Aired** 5 Aug 22.
>**Dir:** Mairzee Almas. **Writ:** Lauren Bello.

7 (1-7) The doll's house
>**prod.** #T13.22357. **Aired** 5 Aug 22.
>**Dir:** Andrés Baiz. **Writ:** Heather Bellson.

8 (1-8) Playing house
>**prod.** #T13.22358. **Aired** 5 Aug 22.
>**Dir:** Andrés Baiz. **Writ:** Alexander Newman-Wise.

9 (1-9) Collectors
>**prod.** #T13.22359. **Aired** 5 Aug 22.
>**Dir:** Coralie Fargeat. **Writ:** Vanessa James Benton.

10 (1-10) Lost hearts
>**prod.** #T13.22360. **Aired** 5 Aug 22.
>**Dir:** Louise Hooper. **Writ:** Jay Franklin.

11 (1-11) A dream of a thousand cats / Calliope
>**prod.** #T13.22361. **Aired** 5 Aug 22.
>**Dir:** Hisko Hulsing & Louise Hooper.
>**Writ:** Catherine Smyth-McMullen.

# PART 4
# DETAILED EPISODE GUIDE

## SHOW CREDITS

Developed by Neil Gaiman, David S. Goyer & Allan Heinberg, based on the DC comic by Neil Gaiman, Sam Kieth & Mike Dringenberg.

End titles by Dave McKean.

Starring Tom Sturridge as Dream/Morpheus, Boyd Holbrook as the Corinthian, Patton Oswalt as the voice of Matthew the raven, Vivienne Acheampong as Lucienne.

Produced by Purepop inc. / Phantom Four / The Blank Corporation / DC / Warner Bros. / Netflix.

All episodes were released on Netflix on August 5, 2022, except for the extra episode au August 19.

## SEASON CREDITS

**Executive producer:** Allan Heinberg, David S. Goyer & Neil Gaiman, with Mike Barker (ep. #1 only).

**Co-executive producers:** Jamie Childs, Austin Guzman, Heather Bellson & Jim Campolongo.

**Supervising producer:** Ameni Rozsa.

**Produced by:** Samson Mücke, with Iain Smith (ep. #1 only).

**Producers:** Alexander Newman-Wise & Andrew Cholerton.

**Line producers:** Damian Anderson (ep. #1 only), Ben Rimmer (eps. #2-3, 5).

**Co-producer:** Vanya Asher.

**Associate producer:** Anya Dubble Olson.

**Story editor:** Lauren Bello.

**Staff writers:** Catherine Smyth-McMullen & Vanessa James Benton.

**Writers' assistant:** Jay Franklin (eps. #1, 11).

**Composer:** David Buckley.

**Music supervisor:** Kasey Truman.

**Cinematographers:** George Steel (eps. #1-2, 5), Sam Heasman (eps. #3-4, 10-11), Will Baldy (eps. #6-9, 11).

**Camera operators:** James Chesterton (eps. #6, 11), John Ferguson (eps. #9-10).

**A camera operator:** Rob Carter (eps. #4, 7-8).

**B camera operator:** Harry Bowers (eps. #1-3, 5).

**Editors:** Daniel Gabbe (eps. #1, 7, 10), Shoshannah Tanzer (eps. #2, 4, 6), Jamin Bricker (eps. #3, 9), Kelly Stuyvesant (eps. #5, 8, 11).

**Additional editing:** Jamin Bricker & Kelly Stuyvesant (ep. #1 only).

**Assistant editors:** Chris Talson (eps. #1, 7, 10), Greg Hollander (eps. #2, 4, 6), Philip Welch (eps. #3, 9), Katharine Neville (eps. #5, 8, 11).

**Production designers:** Gary Steele, with Hisko Hulsing (ep. #11 only).

**Supervising art director:** Nicki McCallum.

**Art directors:** Kevin Timon-Hill (ep. #1), Luke Whitelock (eps. #2, 5, 8), Sandra Phillips (eps. #3, 6, 9), Patsy Johnson (eps. #4, 7, 10-11).

**Set decorators:** Lisa Chugg (eps. #1-3, 5), Liz Griffiths (eps. #4, 6-11).

**Construction manager:** Stuart Watson.

**Costume designer:** Sarah Arthur.

**Assistant costume designer:** Dominique Arthur.

**Costume supervisor:** Ceri Walford.

**Make-up and hair designer:** Graham Johnston.

**Make-up and hair supervisor:** Ann Fenton.

**Visual effects supervisor:** Ian Markiewicz.

**Graphic artist:** Kimberley Bright.

**1st assistant directors:** Chris Carreras (ep. #1), Richard Harris (eps. #2, 6-9, 11), Gareth Tandy (eps. #2-4, 10-11), Martin Curry (ep. #5).

**2nd assistant directors:** Rhys Summerhayes (ep. #1), Anna Brabbins (eps. #2-5, 7-8), Bryn Lawrence (ep. #3), Tom Beacham (eps. #6, 9-11), Charlotte Ellis (eps. #6, 10), Charlotte Miles (ep. #9).

**Casting:** Lucinda Syson & Natasha Vincent.

**Casting associate:** Jenna Bamberger.

**Script supervisor:** Marianne Huet.

**Script coordinator:** Gregory Goetz.

**Dialogue supervisor:** Curt Schulkey.

**Stunt coordinator:** Peter Pedrero.

**Music editors:** Jason Lingle (eps. #1, 3, 5, 7, 9, 11), Jeff Lingle (eps. #2, 4, 6, 8, 10).

**Production sound mixers:** Paul Munro (eps. #1-3, 5, 7-8), Jerome McCann (eps. #4, 6, 9-11).

**Sound assistants:** Alex Bryce (ep. #4), Jeremy Brown (ep. #11).

**1st assistant sound editor:** Ross Adams (ep. #9).

**Key grip:** Andy Woodcock.

**Lighting supervisor:** Niklas Ström (eps. #1-3).

**Gaffers:** Wayne King (eps. #1-2, 5), Bernhard Rostoski (ep. #3), Jack Powell (eps. #4, 6, 9-11), Tim Wiley (eps. #7-8).

**Best boy electric:** Alan Grayley (eps. #2, 7).

**Best boy grip:** Rogan Brown (ep. #2), Ian Ogden (ep. #8).

**Rigging electrics:** Michael Forster (ep. #1), Simon Dutton (eps. #1, 6), Jack Lawlor (ep. #6).

**Rigging gaffer:** John Harris.

**Property master:** Gordon Fitzgerald.

**Assistant property master:** Robert Orr.

**Head greensman:** Jon Marson.

**Supervising location manager:** Casper Mill.

**Location managers:** Mandy Sharpe (eps. #1, 3, 5), Peter Kelly (eps. #2, 4, 6-11).

**Transportation coordinator:** Stevie Kotey.

**Transport co-captain:** Maurice Batson.

**Clearance coordinators:** Gina Cook & Shân Hughes.

**Production controller:** Ann Marie Fitzgerald.

**Production accountant:** Corrine Millson-Crane.

**1st assistant accountant:** Darren Holmes (eps. #2, 7).

**Assistants to the executive producers:** Spencer Soloman, Jo Mance, Rachael Clark, Jake Brown, Marina Marlens, Sarah-Kate Fenelon & Valentina Novakovic.

**Post-production coordinators:** Kevin Pardo (ep. #1), Abbey Jackloski (ep. #2), Fred Kern (eps. #3-11).

**Post-production assistants:** Abbey Jackloski (ep. #1), Emily Kim (eps. #2-11).

**Production managers:** Tony Davis (ep. #1), Lara Dorée & Erin Vitali (eps. #2-11).

**Production supervisor:** Dorothee Freytag (eps. #2-11).

**Production coordinators:** Stuart Ewen & Silvia Felce (ep. #1), Josh Lowe (eps. #2-11).

**Assistant production coordinator:** Zsófia Zatureczki (eps. #5, 10).

# EPISODE CREDITS

## #1 (101) Chapter 1: Sleep of the just

**Directed by:** Mike Barker.

**Teleplay by:** Neil Gaiman, David S. Goyer & Allan Heinberg.

**Guest starring:** Niamh Walsh *as young Ethel Cripps*, Bill Paterson *as Dr. John Hathaway*, Laurie Kynaston *as Alex Burgess*, and Charles Dance *as Sir Roderick Burgess*.

**Co-starring:** Ansu Kabia *as Ruthven Sykes*, Benjamin Evan Ainsworth *as Alex Burgess (6)*, Stacy Abalogun *as nurse Ed-*

*munds*, Nicola Achilleas *as pushy person #4*, Jennifer Adab *as disciple #5*, Roger Ajogbe *as James Kincaid*, Will Atiomo *as guard #4 (Maurice)*, Martin Bishop *as neurologist*, Benedick Blythe *as Alex Burgess (70)*, Alistair Bourne *as pushy person #1*, Ione Brown *as sleepwalking patient*, Clare Buckingham *as sleep-deprived patient*, Andre Bullock *as pushy person #3*, Simon Bundock *as Alex Burgess double (6)*, James Chuma Mbanefo *as guard #5 (Rogers)*, Tracy Collier *as disciple #2*, Christopher Colquhoun *as Paul McGuire (62)*, Naomi Cooper-Davis *as guard #11 (Ernie)*, Sion Alun Davies *as Ozzie*, Keiran Flynn *as taxi driver*, Gus Gordon *as Paul McGuire (18-42)*, Robert Grose *as disciple #1*, Gill Jordan *as disciple #4*, Jordan Long *as guard #10 (Fred)*, Louis Martin *as guard #3 (Noel)*, Corey Mylchreest *as Adonis*, Johnny Palmiero *as guard #2 (Simon)*, Euene Rangayah *as disciple #3*, Amy Rockson *as Margaret Kincaid*, Douglas Russell *as guard #1 (Hugo)*, Madeleine Wilshire *as pushy person #2*, Momo Yeung *as disciple #6*.

While attempting to capture Death, Sir Roderick Burgess captures Dream instead. The Corinthian, an escaped nightmare, tells the British aristocrat of the advantages he could gain from keeping Morpheus prisoner—not least of which, immortality. Except the prisoner refuses to speak or to give anything to anyone. And while he remains trapped, people around the world fall into a never-ending sleep.

## #2 (102) Chapter 2: Imperfect hosts

**Directed by:** Jamie Childs.
**Teleplay by:** Allan Heinberg.

**Guest starring:** Jenna Coleman *as Johanna Constantine,* Joely Richardson *as Ethel Dee,* Niamh Walsh *as young Ethel Cripps,* Sanjeev Bhaskar *as Cain,* Asim Chaudhry *as Abel,* Nina Wadia *as Fate Mother,* Souad Faress *as Fate Crone,* Dinita Gohil *as Fate Maiden,* and David Thewlis *as John Dee.*

**Co-starring:** Ansu Kabia *as Ruthven Sykes,* Graham Bohea *as hangman,* Joe Corrigall *as Sam,* Crystal Yu *as Jackie.*

Finally free after a century of captivity, Morpheus returns to his domain—the Dreaming—only to find his palace in ruins and his kingdom abandoned. Now he must retrieve the three artifacts at the source of his power that were stolen by his captor's mistress when she fled from him decades prior. Only then will he be able to restore his realm to its previous glory.

## #3 (103) Chapter 3: Dream a little dream of me

**Directed by:** Jamie Childs.

**Teleplay by:** Jim Campolongo.

**Guest starring:** Jenna Coleman *as Johanna Constantine,* Joely Richardson *as Ethel Dee,* Meera Syal *as Erica,* Clare Higgins *as Mad Hettie,* and David Thewlis *as John Dee.*

**Co-starring:** Eleanor Fanyinka *as Rachel,* Hannah van der Westhuysen *as the princess,* Stephen Odubola *as Kevin Brody,* Marcus Fraser *as Agilieth,* Stevie Hutchinson *as Alex Logue,* Nina Rose Galano *as Astra Logue,* Olu Adaeze *as armed officer #1,* Marcus Adolphy *as cab driver,* Joe Corrigall *as Sam,* Sam Donnelly *as armed officer #2.*

With the help of Matthew the raven, Morpheus retrieves his pouch of sand from exorcist Johanna Constantine. Meanwhile, the Corinthian warns Ethel Cripps (Burgess' old mistress) that Dream will soon visit her to take back the ruby she stole from him—a ruby her son John is obsessed with.

## #4 (104) Chapter 4: A hope in Hell

**Directed by:** Jamie Childs.

**Teleplay by:** Austin Guzman.

**Guest starring:** Gwendoline Christie *as Lucifer Morningstar*, Sarah Niles *as Rosemary*, Cassie Clare *as Mazikeen of the Lilim*, Martyn Ford *as Squatterbloat*, Munya Chawawa *as Choronzon*, Deborah Oyelade *as Nada*, Ernest Kingsley, Jr. *as Kai'ckul*, Sam Strike *as Todd*, and David Thewlis *as John Dee*.

**Co-starring:** Eleanor Fanyinka *as Rachel*, Hannah van der Westhuysen *as the princess*, Stephen Odubola *as Kevin Brody*, Marcus Fraser *as Agilieth*, Stevie Hutchinson *as Alex Logue*, Nina Rose Galano *as Astra Logue*, Olu Adaeze *as armed officer #1*, Marcus Adolphy *as cab driver*, Joe Corrigall *as Sam*, Sam Donnelly *as armed officer #2*.

After traveling to Hell, Morpheus must confront Lucifer to win back his helm that is currently in the possession of a demon. Meanwhile, a woman helps John and drives him to the place where the ruby is stored. To thank her, he gives her his mother's protective amulet.

# #5 (105) Chapter 5: 24/7

**Directed by:** Jamie Childs.

**Teleplay by:** Ameni Rozsa.

**Guest starring:** Mason Alexander Park *as Desire*, Joely Richardson *as Ethel Dee*, Niamh Walsh *as young Ethel Cripps*, Kyo Ra *as Rose Walker*, Emma Duncan *as Bette Munroe*, Steven Brand *as Marsh Janowski*, Laurie Davidson *as Mark Brewer*, Daisy Head *as Judy*, James Udom *as Garry*, Lourdes Faberes *as Kate Fletcher*, and David Thewlis *as John Dee*.

**Co-starring:** Sarah Quist *as Lindy*, Jennifer Armour *as traffic report Terri*, Kirsten Foster *as news anchor Annie*, Jay Rincon *as meteorologist Mike*, Georgia Goodman *as Rebecca*, Walles Hamonde *as Jeff*.

After recovering the ruby, John enters a diner. Talking to the waitress, he decides to show her and all the patrons what the world would be like if everyone always spoke the truth. The ruby grants him his wish, and people around him begin to kill each other or themselves. Morpheus arrives and transports John into the realm of dreams where the two men clash.

# #6 (106) Chapter 6: The sound of her wings

**Directed by:** Mairzee Almas.

**Teleplay by:** Lauren Bello.

**Guest starring:** Kirby Howell-Baptiste *as Death*, Jenna Coleman *as Johanna Constantine*, Mason Alexander Park *as Desire*, Ferdinand Kingsley *as Hob Gadling*, Samuel Blenkin *as Will Shaxberd*, Ian McNeice *as bartender*.

**Co-starring:** Angus Yellowlees *as Kit Marlowe*, Sarah Twomey *as Lushing Lou*, Curtis Kantsa *as Franklin*, Kieron Moore *as Crispin*, Mark Field *as Roland*, Sia Alipour *as Aiden*, Jon Rumney *as Harry*, Rebecca Night *as Esme*, Leemore Marrett, Jr. *as tourist husband Sam*, Liberty Buckland *as tourist wife Tabitha*, Stanley Morgan *as Charlie*, Harry Burton *as Geoffrey Chaucer*, William Chubb *as Edmund*, Ben Abell *as pub landlord (1389)*, Alex Akindeji *as Louis*, Hannah Zoé Ankrah *as bar patron #1 (1989)*, Archie Backhouse *as bar patron #3 (1989)*, Kevin Brewer *as pub visitor #5 (1389)*, Kylie Butler *as pub visitor #3 (1389)*, Paul Cassidy *as pub visitor #2 (1389)*, Michael Clarke *as bar patron #2 (1989)*, Kelse Cooke *as Tara*, Nigel Cooke *as tavern visitor #1 (1689)*, Nick Cornwall *as pub visitor #1 (1389)*, Zody Daines *as waitress (1989)*, Reanne Farley *as tavern serving maid (1689)*, Aykut Hilmi *as pub visitor #4 (1389)*, Ruchika Jain *as Clara*, Danielle Kassaraté *as tavern waitress (1589)*, Angus Kennedy *as tavern landlord (1789)*, Akil Largie *as bouncer (1689)*, John Leader *as Freddie*, Tony Richardson *as man in the shadows (1689)*, Benjamin Wainwright *as tavern visitor #2 (1689)*.

Dream meets up with his sister, Death. As they walk and talk, he watches her work. The way she guides the dying with so much kindness and compassion moves him and prompts him to seek out an immortal human he has been meeting with once every one hundred years.

Quite possibly the most touching and emotional episode. Beautifully written and performed.

# #7 (107) Chapter 7: The doll's house

**Directed by:** Andrés Baiz.

**Teleplay by:** Heather Bellson.

**Guest starring:** Mason Alexander Park *as Desire*, John Cameron Mitchell *as Hal Carter*, Asim Chaudhry *as Abel*, Kyo Ra *as Rose Walker*, Razane Jammal *as Lyta Hall*, Sandra James-Young *as Unity Kincaid*, Donna Preston *as Despair*, Nina Wadia *as Fate Mother*, Souad Faress *as Fate Crone*, Dinita Gohil *as Fate Maiden*, Lloyd Everitt *as Hector Hall*, Andi Osho *as Miranda Walker*, Cara Horgan *as Chantal*, Lily Travers *as Barbie*, Richard Fleeshman *as Ken*, Daisy Badger *as Zelda*, Jill Winternitz *as The Good Doctor*, Kerry Shale *as Nimrod*, Danny Kirrane *as Fun Land*, Sam Hazeldine *as Barnaby*, Lisa O'Hare *as Clarice*, Ben Wiggins *as Carl*.

**With:** Stephen Fry *as Gilbert*, and Mark Hamill *as the voice of Mervyn Pumpkinhead.*

**Co-starring:** Eddie Karanja *as Jed Walker*, Shelley Williams *as Eleanor Rubio*, Peter de Jersey *as Mr. Holdaway*, Aryel Tsoto *as young Jed Walker*, Nicholas Anscombe *as Merv Pumpkinhead (body)*, Aimée Cassettari *as flight attendant*, Angus Castle-Doughty *as Devin*, Kai Ismail *as teenage waiter*, Charlie Locke *as Trey*, Leo Munby *as pianist.*

After the death of their parents, Rose and Jed were separated. Six years later, Rose tries to find her younger brother. But the girl is a Vortex, capable of affecting dreams in ways that could destroy the Dreaming. Desire and Despair plan to use her against Morpheus. And the Corinthian, too, would like to get his hands on her...

# #8 (108) Chapter 8: Playing house

**Directed by:** Andrés Baiz.

**Teleplay by:** Alexander Newman-Wise.

**Guest starring:** John Cameron Mitchell *as Hal Carter*, Lenny Henry *as the voice of Martin Tenbones*, Kyo Ra *as Rose Walker*, Razane Jammal *as Lyta Hall*, Lloyd Everitt *as Hector Hall*, Sandra James-Young *as Unity Kincaid*, Sam Hazeldine *as Barnaby*, Lisa O'Hare *as Clarice*, Lily Travers *as Barbie*, Richard Fleeshman *as Ken*, Daisy Badger *as Zelda*, Cara Horgan *as Chantal*, Andi Osho *as Miranda Walker*, Ann Ogbomo *as Gault*.

**Co-starring:** Eddie Karanja *as Jed Walker*, Shelley Williams *as Eleanor Rubio*, Isla Gie *as Child Zelda*, Sacharissa Claxton *as Off. Sandra Davis*.

With the help of other guests at the bed & breakfast, Rose starts looking for her brother in Cape Kennedy. Morpheus also agrees to help her. The Corinthian beats them to the punch and, after murdering the boy's foster parents, takes Jed with him to a serial killer convention.

# #9 (109) Chapter 9: Collectors

**Directed by:** Coralie Fargeat.

**Teleplay by:** Vanessa James Benton.

**Guest starring:** Kyo Ra *as Rose Walker*, Razane Jammal *as Lyta Hall*, Sandra James-Young *as Unity Kincaid*, Lloyd Everitt *as Hector Hall*, Lewis Reeves *as Philip Sitz*, Dany Kirrane *as Fun Land*, Jill Winternitz *as The Good Doctor*, Kerry Shale *as Nimrod*.

**With:** Stephen Fry *as Gilbert*, and Mark Hamill *as the voice of Mervyn Pumpkinhead*.

**Co-starring:** Eddie Karanja *as Jed Walker*, Peter de Jersey *as Mr. Holdaway*, Nicholas Anscombe *as Merv Pumpkinhead (body)*, Dickie Beau *as The Shredder*, Zora Bishop *as Myth America*, Desiree Burch *as Grass Widow*, JP Conway *as The Connoisseur*, Jimmy Essex *as Carrion*, Joe Frost *as The Choirboy*, David Menkin *as The Hammer of God*, Laila Pyne *as Albina the reception clerk*, Daniel Quirke *as Moon River*, Kirris Rivieré *as Adonai*, Matthew Sim *as The Crooner*, Daniel Tuite *as Hello Little Girl*, Michael Walters *as The Water Boy*.

Rose's powers grow, threatening to break the wall between the Dreaming and the real world. The Corinthian calls the girl to tell her he found her brother and she drives with Gilbert to the serial killer convention to meet up with them. Gilbert—who really is one of the Dreaming's escaped residents—recognizes the Corinthian for what he truly is and hurries to warn his creator.

## #10 (110) Chapter 10: Lost hearts

**Directed by:** Louise Hooper.
**Teleplay by:** Jay Franklin.
**Guest starring:** Gwendoline Christie *as Lucifer Morningstar*, Mason Alexander Park *as Desire*, John Cameron Mitchell *as Hal Carter*, Lenny Henry *as the voice of Martin Tenbones*, Roger Allam *as the voice of Lord Azazel*, Kyo Ra *as Rose Walker*, Razane Jammal *as Lyta Hall*, Ben Wiggins *as Carl*, Sandra James-Young *as Unity Kincaid*, Ann Ogbomo *as Gault*, Cassie Clare *as Mazikeen of the Lilim*, Lily Travers *as Barbie*, Richard Fleeshman *as Ken*, Cara Horgan *as Chantal*, Daisy Badger *as Zelda*, Jill Winternitz *as The Good Doctor*, Kerry Shale *as Nimrod*, and Stephen Fry *as Gilbert*.

**Co-starring:** Eddie Karanja *as Jed Walker*, Isla Gie *as Child Zelda*, Dickie Beau *as The Shredder*, Zora Bishop *as Myth America*, Desiree Burch *as Grass Widow*, Nalân Burgess *as nurse Sindy*, JP Conway *as The Connoisseur*, Jimmy Essex *as Carrion*, Joe Frost *as The Choirboy*, Alex Harrison *as Hal/Dolly double*, David Menkin *as The Hammer of God*, Daniel Quirke *as Moon River*, Kirris Rivieré *as Adonai*, Matthew Sim *as The Crooner*, Daniel Tuite *as Hello Little Girl*, Michael Walters *as The Water Boy*.

The season reaches its climax at the serial killer convention, where Rose must work with Morpheus to stop the Corinthian then face the uncomfortable truth of her nature and the danger she poses to all the people she loves—including her brother. Dream also uncovers Desire's plot to trick him into breaking a rule of his kin.

# #11 (111) A dream of a thousand cats / Calliope

**Directed by:** Hisko Hulsing *(part 1)* and Louise Hooper *(part 2)*.

**Teleplay by:** Catherine Smyth-McMullen.

**PART 1 – A DREAM OF A THOUSAND CATS (animated)**

**Guest starring:** Sandra Oh *as voice of the cat prophet*, Rosie Day *as voice of the tabby kitten*, David Gyasi *as voice of the grey cat*, Joe Lycett *as voice of the black cat*, Neil Gaiman *as voice of the skull crow*, James McAvoy *as voice of the golden-haired man*, David Tennant *as voice of Don*, Georgia Tennant *as voice of Laura Lynn*, Anna Lundberg *as voice of Marion*, Michael Sheen *as voice of Paul*, Nonso Anozie *as voice of the wyvern*, Diane Morgan *as voice of the gryphon*, Tom Wu *as voice of the pegasus.*

**Co-starring:** Bruno Aversa *as golden haired man (body)*, Nicole Evans *as Marion (body)*, Jeffrey Mundell *as Don (body)*, Mark Osmond *as Paul (body)*, Louise Williams *as Laura Lynn (body)*,

**PART 2 – CALLIOPE**

**Guest starring:** Melissanthi Mahut *as Calliope*, Arthur Darvill *as Richard Madoc*, Nina Wadia *as Fate Mother*, Souad Faress *as Fate Crone*, Dinita Gohil *as Fate Maiden*, Kevin Harvey *as Larry*, Amita Suman *as Nora*, and Derek Jacobi *as Erasmus Fry*.

**Co-starring:** Justina Kehinde *as Sofia*, Kirsty Rider *as Emanuela*, Jessica Murrain *as Alisa*, Hopi Grace *as Lara*, Merch Husey *as Josh*, Fiona Marr *as Erin*, Valmike Rampersad *as Callum*, Yasmeen Scott *as Lottie*, Freddie Stewart *as Elliot*.

Two bonus episodes in one.

The first part is a short 16 minute cartoon where cats discuss how the world once was ruled by them, with humans being their tiny servants until the latter *dreamed* for things to change.

The second tells the story of an uninspired author who keeps a Muse prisoner in his house so he can write more books. But Calliope once was married to Morpheus. So when she reaches out for his help, he is more than willing to step in...

www.ingramcontent.com/pod-product-compliance
Lightning Source LLC
LaVergne TN
LVHW010841200726
843508LV00012B/2686